America's ANIMAL COMEBACKS

Red Wolves

And Then There Were (Almost) None

by Meish Goldish

Consultant: Diane Hendry, Outreach Coordinator
U.S. Fish and Wildlife Service
Red Wolf Recovery Program
Alligator River National Wildlife Refuge

BEARPORT PUBLISHING

New York, New York

Credits

Cover and Title Page, © Valerie Abbott; 4, Courtesy of U.S. Fish and Wildlife Service; 5, Courtesy of U.S. Fish and Wildlife Service; 7, © Sergio Pitamitz/Danita Delimont/Alamy; 8, Courtesy of U.S. Fish and Wildlife Service; 9, © Tom & Pat Leeson; 9T, © Darren Bennett/Animals Animals Enterprises; 9B, © Erwin & Peggy Bauer/Wildstock; 10, Courtesy of U.S. Fish and Wildlife Service; 11, © Joel Sartore Photography; 12, Courtesy of U.S. Fish and Wildlife Service; 13, Courtesy of U.S. Fish and Wildlife Service; 14, © Joel Sartore Photography; 15, © William Munoz; 16, Courtesy of U.S. Fish and Wildlife Service; 17, © Stouffer Productions/Animals Animals Enterprises; 18, © Mark Newman/ Bruce Coleman Inc.; 19, © Jane Faircloth/Transparencies, Inc.; 20, © John and Karen Hollingsworth; 21L, Courtesy of U.S. Fish and Wildlife Service; 21R, © Joel Sartore/ Grant Heilman Photography; 22, Courtesy of U.S. Fish and Wildlife Service; 23, © Ron Buskirk/Alamy; 24, Courtesy of U.S. Fish and Wildlife Service; 25, Tom Brakefield/ Corbis; 27, © Barbara Von Hoffmann/Animals Animals Enterprises; 28, © Robert Winslow/Animals Animals Enterprises; 29T, © Ottfried Schreiter/imagebroker/Alamy; 29B, © Martin Harvey/Corbis; 31, © Jane Faircloth/Transparencies, Inc.

Publisher: Kenn Goin
Senior Editor: Lisa Wiseman
Creative Director: Spencer Brinker
Photo Researcher: Amy Dunleavy
Design: Dawn Beard Creative

Library of Congress Cataloging-in-Publication Data

Goldish, Meish.
 Red wolves : and then there were (almost) none / by Meish Goldish.
    p. cm. — (America's animal comebacks)
 Includes bibliographical references and index.
 ISBN-13: 978-1-59716-742-0 (library binding)
 ISBN-10: 1-59716-742-8 (library binding)
 1. Red wolf—Conservation—United States—Juvenile literature. 2. Endangered species—United States—Juvenile literature. I. Title.

QL737.C22G596 2009
333.95'97730973—dc22

                          2008030831

For more information, write to Bearport Publishing Company, Inc., 101 Fifth Avenue, Suite 6R, New York, New York, 10003. Printed in the United States of America.

10 9 8 7 6 5 4 3 2 1

Contents

Big Questions 4

Changing Times 6

Getting Smaller 8

Catching Wolves 10

Real Reds 12

A New Home 14

Branching Out 16

The Right Spot 18

Getting Ready 20

Losses and Gains 22

New Thinking 24

The Future 26

Red Wolf Facts 28

Other Wolves in Danger 29

Glossary 30

Bibliography 31

Read More 31

Learn More Online 31

Index 32

About the Author 32

Big Questions

It was an important day for the **biologists** at the Alligator River National Wildlife **Refuge** in North Carolina. They were about to let a pair of red wolves known as 140M and 231F go free. They were the first of eight red wolves to be **released** into the **wild**.

Many people greeted the red wolves when
they arrived in North Carolina.

While excited about the release of the wolves, the biologists were also nervous. The eight adult wolves had spent all their lives in **captivity**. They had been raised and fed by people. Would they know how to hunt on their own? Could they raise **pups** in the wild? With no other wolves to help them, would these eight animals be able to survive?

The biologists released the red wolves on September 14, 1987. Before they were set free, there were no red wolves living anywhere in the wild.

The adult wolves ranged in age from three to six years old.

Changing Times

Thousands of years ago, two million wolves roamed freely across North America. About 100,000 of them were red wolves. Their territory stretched from what is now Texas to Florida and as far north as Maine. During this time, the wolves lived mostly in peace among the Native Americans.

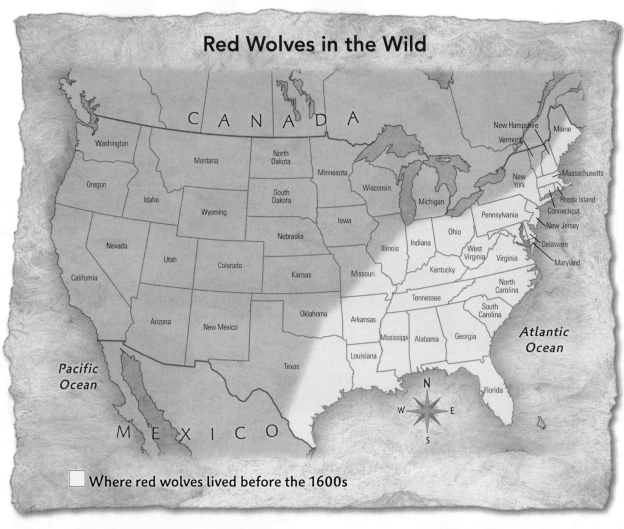

Red Wolves in the Wild

☐ Where red wolves lived before the 1600s

Some scientists think red wolves may have once lived as far north as Canada.

Things changed, however, when European settlers came to America in the 1600s. They feared wolves. The popular fairy tale "Little Red Riding Hood" warned children about a "big bad wolf" that ate people. Farmers hated wolves because they attacked their sheep and other livestock. As a result, people began to kill them. The killings went on for hundreds of years. By the 1960s, red wolves were nearly **extinct**. Only about 17 remained in the wild.

Red wolves are shy animals. They are afraid of people and try to avoid them. There is no record of a healthy red wolf ever attacking a person.

Little Red Riding Hood and the "Big Bad Wolf"

Getting Smaller

In the 1960s, a scientist named Howard McCarley was studying red wolves in the wild. He was surprised to find that many of them were **breeding** with coyotes because they couldn't find other red wolves to **mate** with. The wolves and coyotes were producing **hybrids**. These animals looked a lot like red wolves. It was hard to tell a pure red wolf from a hybrid.

Howard McCarley studied red wolves for more than ten years, starting in the 1950s.

McCarley's discovery led him to believe that there were even fewer pure red wolves in the wild than anyone thought. He feared that they would become extinct.

Another scientist, Ronald Nowak, agreed with him. Nowak asked wildlife officials to **ban** the hunting of red wolves. Officials felt, however, that there were more red wolves than the scientists claimed. They let the killing of the animals continue.

coyote

red wolf

hybrid

A red wolf is normally larger than a coyote. A hybrid can be similar in size and appearance to a red wolf, though it sometimes has broader shoulders and a wider head.

Catching Wolves

As hunting continued, there were fewer and fewer red wolves. By 1969, these animals could be found only along the coasts of Texas and Louisiana. Their **habitat**, which was near dirty, bug-filled water, was unhealthy. Some adult wolves and their pups died from worms that entered their bodies through mosquito bites and then harmed their hearts. Other wolves had mange (MAYNJ), a skin disease transmitted from wolf to wolf that made their fur fall out. There was also little food for wolves to eat in this unhealthy habitat.

A red wolf suffering from mange

Finally, wildlife officials realized that red wolves were in trouble. They decided the best way to help the animals was to catch all the pure red wolves and breed them in captivity. They rounded up all the animals in Texas and Louisiana that looked like red wolves. In seven years, about 400 animals were captured. The last red wolf was caught in 1980. Red wolves were now considered extinct in the wild.

Soft-sided leg traps allow red wolves to be captured without harming them.

soft-sided leg trap

The Red Wolf Recovery Program began in 1973. Its aim is to increase the number of red wolves.

Real Reds

Wildlife officials now faced a big problem. They wanted to breed only pure red wolves. Yet the 400 animals they caught looked nearly the same. Which were pure red wolves, and which were coyotes or hybrids? Biologists had to **analyze** each animal's size, shape, and weight.

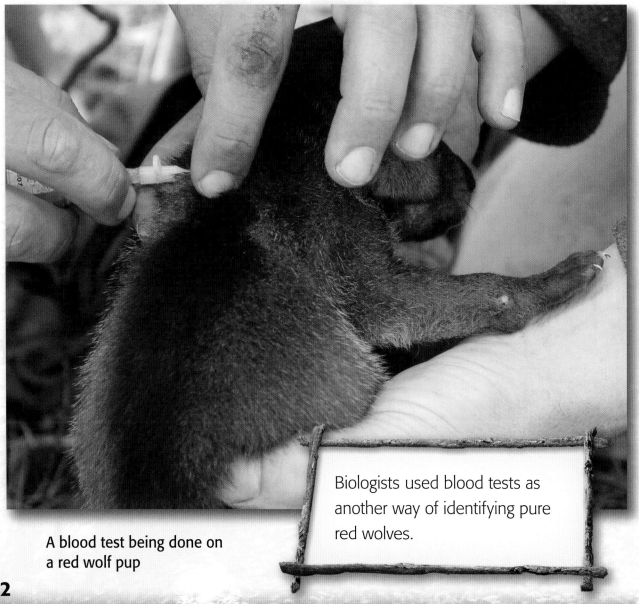

A blood test being done on a red wolf pup

Biologists used blood tests as another way of identifying pure red wolves.

One way that biologists tested the animals was by measuring their skulls. They compared them to the skulls of known red wolves. They also listened to each animal's howl to hear if it sounded like a red wolf howl.

It took six years to test all 400 animals. In the end, scientists were shocked. Only 17 of them were found to be pure red wolves.

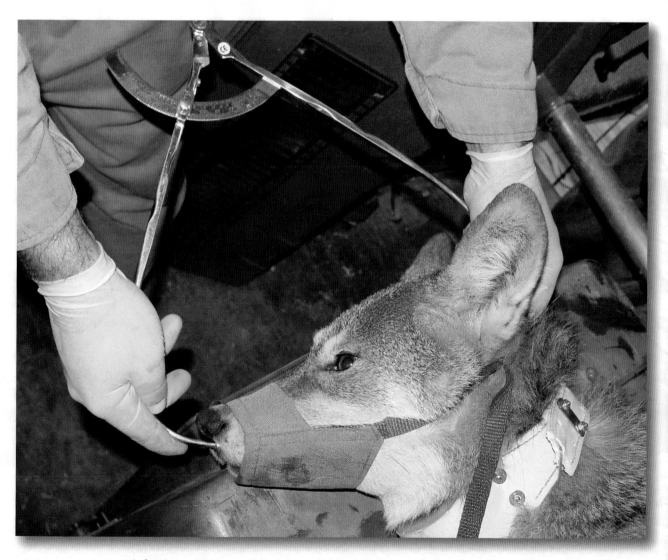

Biologists measured the length and width of the animals' skulls.
The skull of a red wolf is wider than that of a coyote.

A New Home

Scientists began breeding red wolves in captivity even before the last of the captive **canines** was tested. In the 1970s, **breeding pens** were built at the Port Defiance Zoo and Aquarium in Tacoma, Washington. Each pen was large enough to hold two red wolves—one male and one female.

Wolves in a breeding pen at the Port Defiance Zoo in Washington

Inside every pen, there was a grassy area where the wolves could move around. Each pen also had a **den** filled with straw where the animals could stay dry and comfortable. Pans held food and water for them. To keep the wolves from escaping, a high fence was built around the pen. Chains were also buried underground to stop the wolves from digging tunnels to escape.

Scientists decided to breed red wolves in Washington State because the kind of worm that can enter and harm an animal's heart did not exist there.

Pens like this one were used to house the red wolves at the Port Defiance Zoo in Washington.

Branching Out

Scientists didn't know if the captive red wolves would breed in their pens. The animals were used to being in the wild. Also, some were old and weak. However, in 1977, a **litter** of pups was born at the Port Defiance Zoo. Soon, more pups were born there. By 1980, the zoo had more than 50 pure red wolves.

A litter of newborn red wolves usually has three to five pups.

Red wolves give birth once a year, either in April or May.

Scientists were happy, yet they were concerned. They felt it was risky to breed the wolves at just one zoo. If a disease broke out there, all the wolves might die. So two more locations were created where red wolves could raise families. In 1980, one was built at the Audubon Zoological Park in Louisiana. The other one was completed in 1981 at the Wild Canid Survival and Research Center in Missouri. Today there are 40 locations where red wolves can breed in captivity.

A red wolf pup weighs less than one pound (454 g) at birth.

The Right Spot

The captive red wolf **population** continued to grow. Officials wanted to release some pairs of wolves into the wild, so the animals could live freely. Yet finding a good **site** was not easy. Red wolf pairs don't like other red wolves in their territory. The area had to be large enough so that each pair of wolves would not enter the territory of other wolves. It needed to have enough **prey** and **shelter** for the animals, too.

Officials planned to release the red wolves in pairs, which included a male and female, so they would breed in the wild.

Red wolves, like other canines, use body wastes to mark the boundaries of their territories. When other wolves find the marks, they know to stay away.

The site also had to be far from farms and ranches with livestock. When land in Tennessee and Kentucky was suggested, farmers and ranchers there **protested**. They feared the wolves would kill their animals. Wildlife groups protested, too. They said too many hunters and coyotes lived in these areas. Finally, in 1984, the Alligator River National Wildlife Refuge in North Carolina was picked as the release site.

Land in northeast North Carolina was chosen as the release site because few people lived there. The area was also large and had enough small prey, such as mice, raccoons, nutria, and rabbits, for the wolves.

Getting Ready

Eight red wolves were chosen to be released into the wild. In 1986, they were brought to North Carolina. The wolves stayed in **acclimation pens** for ten months to get used to the area before being released. At first they were fed dog food and dead animals. Later they were given live animals to help them get used to hunting.

A red wolf in an acclimation pen

While in the acclimation pens, biologists put collars that contained radio transmitters on the animals. Each transmitter produced its own **unique** signal. Biologists would be able to track each animal's movement in the wild by listening to the signals given off by its collar.

A biologist listening to radio signals given off by the wolves' collars

The collars put on the wolves were called radio collars.

Losses and Gains

In 1987, the eight red wolves were finally released. Sadly, most didn't do well in the North Carolina wild. 231F died from bleeding inside her body. Biologists do not know the cause. 140M and another wolf were hit and killed by cars. One wolf choked to death while eating a raccoon. Two others were badly hurt or killed while fighting with other wolves.

A red wolf in the wild

While these events were sad, officials still felt the release was a success. Why? A female wolf named 205F gave birth in the wild. More pups followed. Then other red wolves were released, and they produced new litters. By 1993, there were more than 50 red wolves living in the wild.

As red wolves filled the wild, more land in North Carolina was set aside for them.

The red wolf is the first **predator** ever to return to the wild after becoming extinct there.

New Thinking

The Red Wolf Recovery Program had great success in **restoring** red wolves to the wild. By the mid-1990s, there were lots of pure red wolves roaming free. With their increased population, people began to realize how important these animals are to the **ecosystem**.

Today, the Red Wolf Recovery Program is used as a model for returning other **endangered** animals to the wild.

Red wolves help to keep the correct balance of plants and animals in their habitat. For example, they eat sick and weak deer in the wild. Once these sick animals are gone, the risk of disease is lower for other animals and there is more food left for the healthy deer. Red wolves also eat animals, such as raccoons, that attack birds' nests. This helps the birds and their chicks survive.

Red wolves help balance the number of animals in the wild and make a better life for many of them.

The Future

The future for red wolves looks good. Today, about 100 to 130 of these animals live in the North Carolina wild. Another 200 are being raised in zoos across the United States. Wildlife officials hope there will be even more wolves in the years ahead. They would like to see at least 220 red wolves in the wild and 330 in captivity at all times.

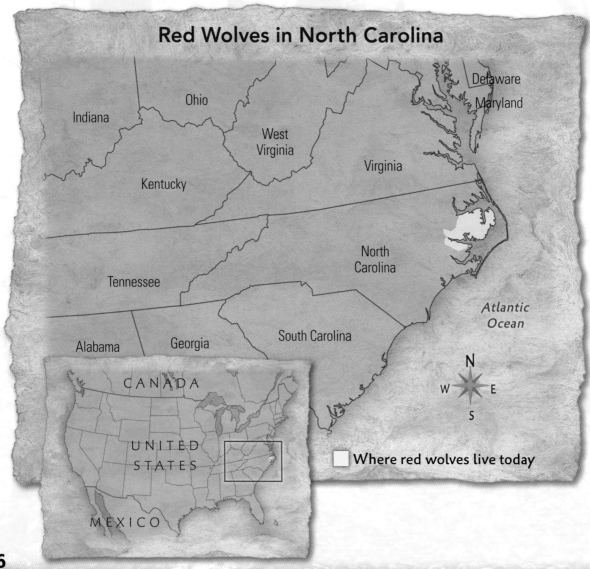

Red Wolves in North Carolina

Delaware
Maryland
Ohio
Indiana
West Virginia
Virginia
Kentucky
North Carolina
Tennessee
Atlantic Ocean
Alabama
Georgia
South Carolina
CANADA
UNITED STATES
MEXICO

☐ Where red wolves live today

N
W E
S

Problems still exist, however. The biggest dangers are red wolves being killed by guns or cars. Also, breeding with coyotes is again hurting the population of red wolves. Wildlife officials are working to solve these problems. If they succeed, red wolves will soon fill new territories in North America.

Today, red wolves live in the wild on 1.7 million acres (687,965 hectares) of land in northeastern North Carolina.

Red Wolf Facts

In 1973, Congress passed the Endangered **Species** Act. This law protects animals and plants that are in danger of dying out in the United States. Harmful activities, such as hunting, capturing, or collecting endangered species, are illegal under this act.

The red wolf was one of the first species listed under the Endangered Species Act. Here are some other facts about the red wolf.

North American population
in 1600: about 100,000
today: about 320

Height
2.2 feet (.6 m) tall at the shoulder

Length
4.6–5.4 feet (1.4–1.6 m) long, including the tail

Weight
50–80 pounds (23–36 kg)

Fur Color
mostly brown and tan, some black and red

Food
white-tailed deer, raccoons, nutria, rabbits, and mice

Life Span
about 7 years in the wild; up to 15 years in captivity

Present Habitat
northeastern North Carolina

Other Wolves in Danger

The red wolf is one kind of wolf that's making a comeback by increasing its numbers. Other types of wolves are also trying to make a comeback.

Gray Wolf

- There are about 200,000 gray wolves in the world. There were once two million in North America alone.

- About 65,000 gray wolves live in North America, mostly in Canada. About 13,000 live in the United States, including Alaska.

- The gray wolf is the largest member of the canine family.

- Today, gray wolves have been reintroduced into Yellowstone National Park in the western United States. Before 1995, there had been no gray wolves there for almost 70 years.

Ethiopian Wolf

- There are only about 550 Ethiopian wolves in the world.

- These animals are sometimes called Abyssinian wolves.

- They live in a country in northeastern Africa called Ethiopia.

- It is illegal to hunt Ethiopian wolves.

- Half of the Ethiopian wolf population lives in Bale Mountain National Park in southern Ethiopia.

Glossary

acclimation pens (*ak*-luh-MAY-shun PENZ) fenced-in areas where animals are kept to give them time to get used to new surroundings

analyze (AN-uh-*lize*) to study something carefully in order to understand it

ban (BAN) to not allow

biologists (bye-OL-uh-jists) scientists who study animals or plants

breeding (BREED-ing) producing young

breeding pens (BREED-ing PENZ) fenced-in areas where animals are kept in order to produce young

canines (KAY-ninez) members of the dog family

captivity (kap-TIV-uh-*tee*) places where animals live in which they are cared for by people, and which are not the animals' natural environments

den (DEN) a hidden place where animals sleep or have babies

ecosystem (EE-koh-*siss*-tuhm) a community of animals and plants that depend on one another to live

endangered (en-DAYN-jurd) being in danger of dying out

extinct (ek-STINGKT) when a kind of plant or animal has died out

habitat (HAB-uh-*tat*) a place in nature where an animal lives

hybrids (HYE-bridz) young that have been bred from two different kinds of animals or plants

litter (LIT-ur) a group of baby animals born at the same time to the same mother

mate (MATE) to come together to produce young

population (*pop*-yuh-LAY-shun) the number of people or animals living in a place

predator (PRED-uh-tur) an animal that hunts other animals for food

prey (PRAY) animals that are hunted or caught for food

protested (PROH-test-id) objected to something in public

pups (PUPS) baby wolves

refuge (REF-yooj) a place that protects animals or people

released (ri-LEEST) set free

restoring (ri-STOR-ing) bringing something back to its original condition

shelter (SHEL-tur) trees, logs, shrubs, rocks, or other parts of a habitat that provide a safe home for a wild animal

site (SITE) a specific area of land

species (SPEE-sheez) groups that animals are divided into, according to similar characteristics

unique (yoo-NEEK) one of a kind; like no other

wild (WILDE) outdoor areas where animals can live and travel freely

Bibliography

Imbriaco, Alison. *The Red Wolf: Help Save This Endangered Species!* Berkeley Heights, NJ: Enslow Publishers (2008).

Parker, Barbara Keevil. *North American Wolves.* Minneapolis, MN: Carolrhoda Books (1998).

Patent, Dorothy Hinshaw. *Gray Wolf, Red Wolf.* New York: Clarion Books (1990).

Silverstein, Alvin, Virginia Silverstein, and Robert Silverstein. *The Red Wolf.* Brookfield, CT: Millbrook Press (1994).

Smith, Roland. *Journey of the Red Wolf.* New York: Dutton (1996).

Read More

Harrington, Fred H. *The Red Wolf.* New York: PowerKids Press (2002).

Havard, Christian. *The Wolf, Night Howler.* Watertown, MA: Charlesbridge (2006).

Hirschi, Ron. *When the Wolves Return.* New York: Dutton (1995).

Markle, Sandra. *Wolves.* Minneapolis, MN: Carolrhoda Books (2004).

Learn More Online

To learn more about red wolves, visit
www.bearportpublishing.com/AnimalComebacks

Index

acclimation pens 20

Alligator River National Wildlife Refuge 4, 19

Audubon Zoological Park 17

breeding pens 14–15, 16

collars 21

coyotes 8–9, 12–13, 19, 27

deer 25, 28

ecosystem 24

Ethiopian wolf 29

Florida 6

gray wolf 29

howling 13

hybrids 8–9, 12

Kentucky 19

Louisiana 10–11, 17

Maine 6

mange 10

McCarley, Howard 8–9

Missouri 17

Native Americans 6

North Carolina 4, 19, 20, 22–23, 26–27, 28

Nowak, Ronald 9

Port Defiance Zoo and Aquarium 14–15

pups 5, 10, 12, 16–17, 23

radio transmitters 21

Red Wolf Recovery Program 11, 24

skulls 13

Tennessee 19

Texas 6, 10–11

Washington 14–15

Wild Canid Survival and Research Center 17

About the Author

Meish Goldish has written more than 100 books for children. His books *Florida Manatees: Warm Water Miracles* and *Gray Wolves: Return to Yellowstone* were recommended by the National Science Teachers Association in 2008.